KW-198-139

938

Ancient Greece Resource Book

Contents

The First Greeks

The Palace of King Minos

There is an ancient Greek story which storytellers
used to tell. It was about a terrible monster called the Minotaur
with the head and horns of a bull and the body of a man.
The storytellers said it lived in a maze under the
palace of King Minos on the island of Crete until an Athenian
prince called Theseus managed to kill it.

For over three thousand years everyone thought this was just a story. No one thought that King Minos was a real person, that there was once a real palace on Crete or a real monster like the Minotaur.

However, nearly a hundred years ago an archaeologist called Arthur Evans heard that someone had found some very old walls on a hill in Crete. He began to dig until he found the remains of an enormous palace.

This shows one of the first rooms that Arthur Evans found. It is the King's Throne Room. Find the throne. The photograph is in black and white because colour film had not been invented in 1900.

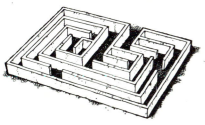

Maze

A set of tunnels or pathways. If you go inside it is sometimes difficult to find your way out.

Archaeologist

Someone who finds out about the past from clues buried under the ground.

Remember that the old stories said that the Minotaur monster was half human and half bull. Arthur Evans and his helpers found pictures of bulls all over the palace.

Arthur Evans found part of this wall painting in the palace. The dark blue parts are ancient. An artist used them as clues to fill in the rest.

The painting shows men and women jumping over a bull. Can you work out how they are doing it?

Arthur Evans decided to rebuild as much of the palace as he could. He and his helpers used the clues they found to work out what the rooms once looked like and what paintings used to be on the walls.

They rebuilt the Throne Room like this with make-believe animals called griffins on the wall.

MIDDLE MINOAN I–III

This Bull's head carved out of stone was in the palace too. The people who lived in the palace may have used it as an altar.

Altar

People often pray to their gods in front of an altar.

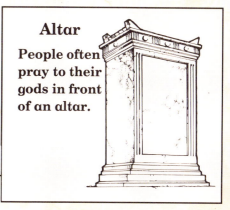

He also found lots of pictures of two-sided axes in the palace.

One was painted on the side of this big jar. People used to keep wine, olive oil and grain for making bread in the jars. The jars were kept in a special store room.

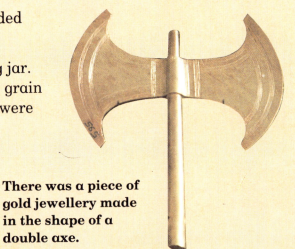

There was a piece of gold jewellery made in the shape of a double axe.

There were more painted on the palace wall. Arthur Evans kept trying to puzzle out what they were there for. Suddenly he had an idea. To understand his idea you will have to learn some Greek words.

The Greek word for double axe is labrys
The Greek word labyrinth means House of the Double Axe.
A labyrinth is another word for maze, the place where the old storytellers said the Minotaur lived.

Arthur Evans thought he had found the palace where the Minotaur had lived. The palace was very big and difficult for people to find their way round.

He had not found anything to say that the story was true, but he had found where some of the first Greeks lived. He also understood a little bit more about the stories they told each other.

The palace was called Knossos. People who lived there are the first ancient Greeks we know much about. We call them the Minoans, after King Minos.

Look at some more clues which the archaeologists have found in Crete.

This gold brooch is made in the shape of two bees. They are putting a drop of honey into a honey comb. The brooch is about three thousand five hundred years old.

This is a little statue of a goddess. She is holding a snake in each hand. Perhaps the people in the palace thought that snakes in the house brought good luck.

Look at all the clues from the palace of Knossos.
How much can you find out from the clues about the people who lived there all that time ago?

The City of Mycenae

Some more wonderful clues have been found about the early ancient Greeks. These were not from Knossos but from a place called Mycenae on the mainland of Greece. We sometimes call them the Myceneans.

This is the gate into the city of Mycenae.

Six graves were also found in Mycenae. Inside were the bodies of nineteen people. There were eight men, nine women and two children. The dead kings were buried with gold masks and weapons. The dead women were wearing golden crowns and rich jewels.

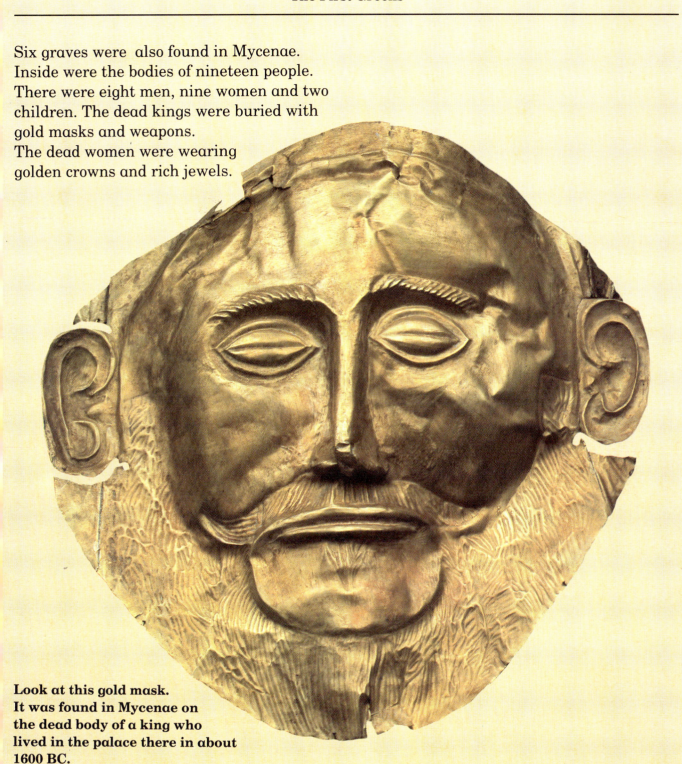

Look at this gold mask. It was found in Mycenae on the dead body of a king who lived in the palace there in about 1600 BC.

This dagger was found in the graves. It has pictures of the River Nile in Egypt on it. What does this tell us about the Myceneans?

The Greek Cities

Athens

Athens is the capital of Greece.
It is very famous because of the people who lived
there in ancient times. They were always asking questions
and trying to find out how things work.
They were very clever artists and they put up
beautiful buildings. People still try to copy them today.

Here are the remains of some of their buildings.

There was no country called 'Greece' in those days. Most Greek people lived on farms in the countryside near a city. They felt that they belonged to that city. They thought of the Greeks who belonged to other cities as different.

There were hundreds of these cities. Most of them were quite small so the people knew each other.

Different cities were ruled in different ways but in nearly all of them the people had the right to choose their leaders. The people in each city were very proud that outsiders could not tell them what to do.

Ancient times
A very long time ago indeed.

This is the Assembly place where the people of Athens had to come to vote for their leaders and to discuss how to run the city.

If the leaders wanted to do something, they always had to ask the people to agree to it first. Anyone who wanted to make a speech had to go up the steps and stand on the platform. Everyone had the right to do this.

The Athenians were proud that the people ruled their city. The people in Athens had more power than people in other Greek cities. But when the Athenians said 'the people', they did not mean everybody. They meant grown up men who were not slaves. Slaves were not allowed to go to the Assembly and vote. Nor were children. Nor were women.

Slaves
People who had to work for other people without having any wages. They could be sold by their owners to someone else.

The Athenians had a way of dealing with anyone who was becoming too powerful. The citizens had to write down the names of any person they thought should leave the city. If six thousand of them wrote the same name that person had to go away for ten years.

They wrote the names on pieces of broken pot like these. Can you read the names?

Sparta

The Greek cities often quarrelled and fought wars with each other. The city that was best at fighting was Sparta.

Sparta was very different from Athens. For one thing it was ruled by two kings.

When boys were seven they were taken from their families to start training to be soldiers. Spartan men had their meals together in special army rooms.

Citizens had to be full-time soldiers. Slaves did all their other work for them.

The Spartans thought old people were important. They chose thirty old men to help to rule the city.

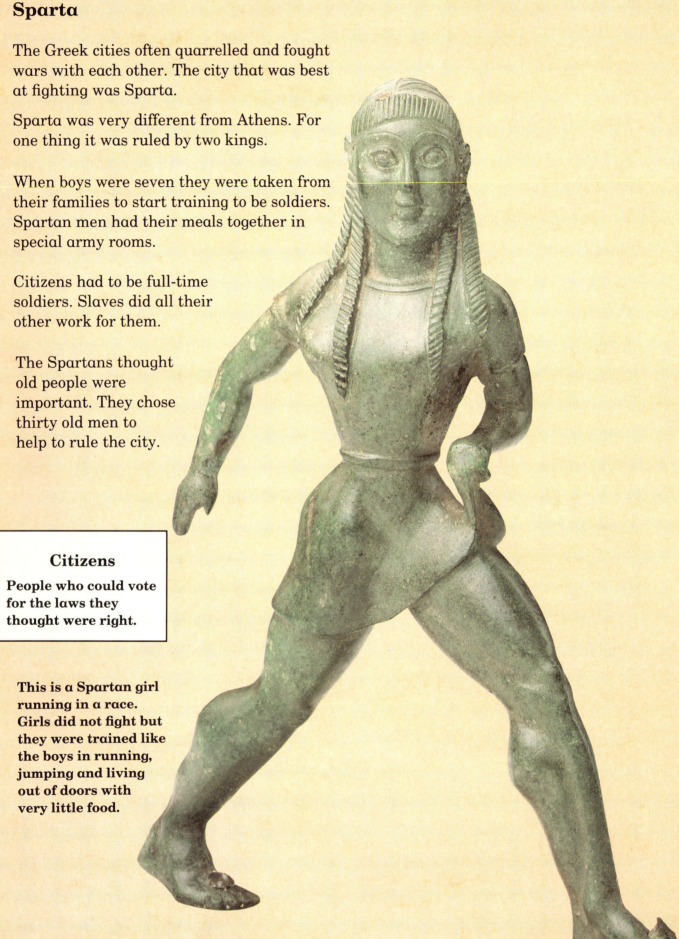

Citizens

People who could vote for the laws they thought were right.

This is a Spartan girl running in a race. Girls did not fight but they were trained like the boys in running, jumping and living out of doors with very little food.

Greek Armies

Greek men between the ages of eighteen and sixty had to be ready to fight for their city.

Whenever the order came they left their farms and workshops. Each one took his helmet and armour down from their place on the wall and started to put them on.

He took his shield, sword and spear and asked the gods for good luck.

Then he said goodbye to his family and went out to join the others.

This picture of a battle between two Greek armies comes from a plate made in the city of Corinth. What does it tell you about their weapons and armour and how they fought their battles?

A Famous Battle

When the Persian king, Xerxes, threatened their cities, the Greeks stopped quarrelling and joined together. What happened next is one of their most famous true stories.

A Spartan king, called Leonidas, chose three hundred of Sparta's best soldiers. Men from the other Greek cities joined them as they marched north towards the mountains that stood between them and the Persians.

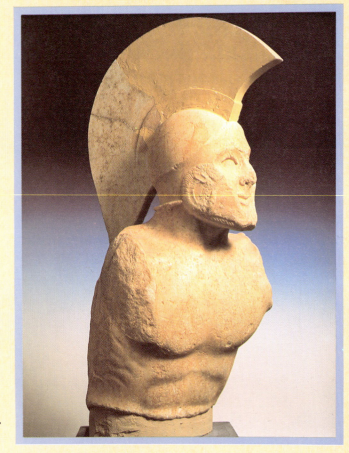

The Spartan King Leonidas.

The Greek plan was simple. There was only one place in the mountains where the Persians could get through. It was a narrow gap, or pass, called Thermopylae.

If the Greeks could hold this pass, the Persians would not be able to get any further.

The Pass of Thermopylae.

When Xerxes arrived he could not believe what he saw.
The Greeks had built a wall across the pass. Some of the Spartans were doing exercises in front of it. Others were carefully combing their long hair which they always did when they were about to risk their lives in battle.

Xerxes thought they were mad. They only had four thousand men. He had two hundred thousand. They must know that they were going to be killed. He waited for them to go home but after four days they were still there. Xerxes got angry. He ordered his soldiers to attack.

The Spartans stood shoulder to shoulder in the narrow pass. The Persians fought for two days. Then they gave up until a man came to Xerxes and said he knew of a secret path that led over the back of the hills and which would take them behind the Greek army. He offered to show the Persians the way if the king would pay him. A group of Persians set out that night. By morning they were looking down at the Greeks below.

This is a statue of a Spartan soldier wearing his helmet and cloak. Can you see his long hair?

When Leonidas saw them he told the Greeks from the other cities to escape while they could. But he and his three hundred Spartans stayed to fight to the end.

As the sun rose Xerxes ordered his men to attack. The Spartans came out from behind the wall and fought so furiously that they soon broke all their spears. They fought on with swords, and then with hands and teeth.

When the Persians came down from the path and attacked them from behind they stood together in a circle on a small hill in the middle of the pass. There, fighting to the last, they were all killed.

Later the Greeks put up a stone to mark the spot where the Spartans had died. On it they wrote,

GO TELL THE
SPARTANS,
YOU WHO READ:
WE TOOK THEIR ORDERS
AND ARE DEAD.

The Greeks and The Sea

Warships

The Greeks were good shipbuilders and sailors.
Their best warship was called a 'trireme'. It was the fastest
and most up-to-date ship of its time.

This is a trireme at sea near Athens in 1987.
It is a copy of those built in ancient times.

A trireme was rowed by a hundred and seventy men. They sat in three rows, one above the other, on each side of the ship.

A trireme was like a floating spear. It had a sharp piece of metal on the front like a knife. Above that was a painted eye.

The idea was to row as fast as possible towards an enemy ship and ram the knife into it so that it sank.

Sometimes soldiers stood on the decks above the rowers so that they could jump onto enemy ships and capture them.

For hundreds of years no one could work out how the Greeks had built triremes. Then, a few years ago, a professor and a ship designer from England managed to solve the puzzle.

They used clues from ancient times like this picture carved on a piece of marble.

The Greeks also fought in ships like this one painted on a vase.

Find:

■ The ram at the front
■ The steering oar
■ The rowers

How is this ship different from a trireme?

The Battle of Salamis

This is the true story of the most famous sea battle that the Greeks fought.

After the Persian king, Xerxes, had defeated the Greeks at the mountain pass of Thermopylae he marched to Athens. The Athenians were very frightened.

The day before the Persians arrived most of them left the city and went to the nearby island of Salamis where the Greek fleet was in harbour.

The Persians had their ships out at sea.

This is the view from the island of Salamis looking back across the water to the mainland. The letter P at the top shows you where the Persian fleet was out at sea. The Greek fleet was hidden in a bay at point G.

The Persians had the most ships but the Greeks decided to trick them. If they could make them go to the narrow strip of water between the island and the mainland the Persian ships would bump into each other.

Pretend you are the Greek leader. How would you trick the Persians into sailing into the trap?

This is what really happened.

The Greeks sent a messenger to the Persians. He pretended to be a traitor and told them that the Greeks were going to try to escape by sailing away in the night. "Don't let them slip through your fingers", he said.

So that night the Persians sent some of their ships round one side of Salamis, while the rest blocked off the channel on the other. They stayed awake all night, paddling to keep their ships in a line across the water, watching for the Greeks who never came.

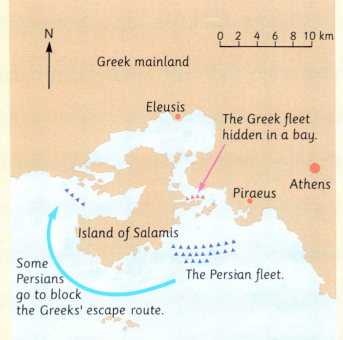

In the morning Xerxes had his throne put up on the mainland looking over the water to Salamis. There he sat down to watch the battle. His soldiers lined the beach ready to kill the Greek sailors as they struggled ashore from their wrecked ships.

Then the Persian fleet moved slowly into the narrow channel.

The Greeks were waiting, hidden in the bay. As the enemy went past they rowed out and smashed into them. The leading Greek ship sliced the back clean off its opponent. Soon the Persians were in trouble. They jammed together and crashed into each other with their own rams. The sea became a mass of wrecks and bodies.

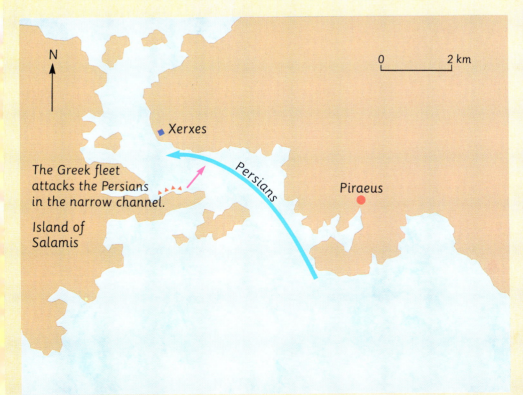

Xerxes saw two hundred of his ships sunk and fifty thousand of his men killed. He ordered what was left of his fleet to sail away and his army to go back the way it had come.

Greek Traders

Here are some clues to tell us about how the Greeks traded with other countries and which countries they went to. They used ships to carry goods to trade with other people.

This Greek painting shows a scene in North Africa near Egypt. A king is watching his workers weigh goods and store them.

Find the scales and the underground storage place.

How many different animals and birds can you see?

Do you think the artist could have painted this without going there?

Archaeologists say this painting shows that the Greeks went to North Africa. Why do you think they say that? Does it prove it?

This photograph was taken under water in modern times.

Find the diver.

He is looking at the wreck of a Greek ship. It was carrying large jars. The Greeks used them to store things like corn, olive oil and wine.

Archaeologists found this wreck near the south coast of France. Does it prove that the Greeks went there?

This ship is being attacked by a pirate ship.
The pirates hope that there is a valuable cargo on board.

This is what pirates liked. It is a jar made of gold and silver. It was made in Greece. Archaeologists found it in Russia.

This coin comes from a Greek colony in Italy. The picture on the front shows what the city was famous for selling.
What is it?
Why would other people in Greek cities be pleased to buy it?

Make a list of places where the Greek traders went, using the clues to help you.

Colony

The Greeks often found there were too many people living in their city and that there was not enough food for them all. So some moved away to a new land and formed a new city. The new city was called a colony.

Everyday Life and Work

Babies and children

Rich families in Ancient Greece had a
nurse to help look after the baby.

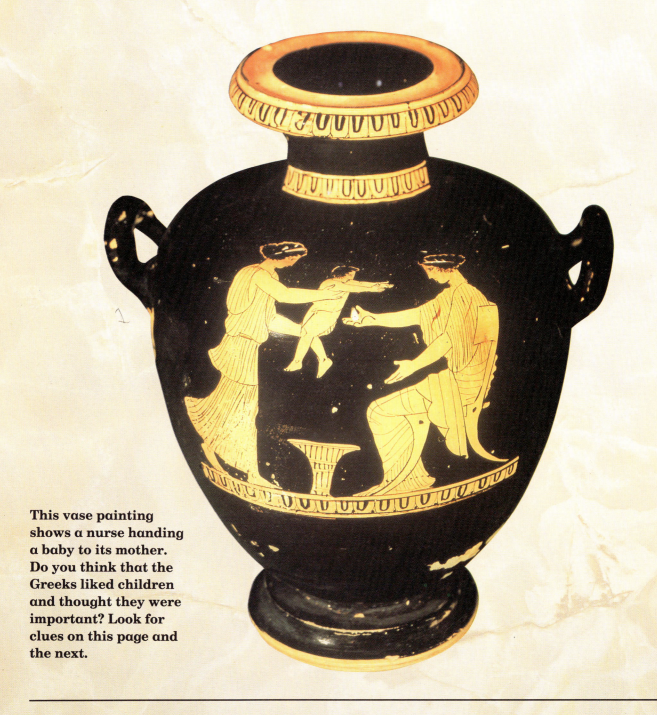

This vase painting
shows a nurse handing
a baby to its mother.
Do you think that the
Greeks liked children
and thought they were
important? Look for
clues on this page and
the next.

Here is a nurse in a Greek play talking about her job:

> I brought him up. Took him new-born from
>   his mother's arms.
>
> And oh! The times he shouted at me in the night,
>
> Made me get up, and bothered me with this and that.
>
> A baby in a cradle can't explain what the matter is,
>
> Whether it wants to eat, to drink, or to make water.
>
> Well, often I could tell; and often too, I know,
>
> I guessed it wrong; and then I'd have to
>   wash his things.

These toys belonged to Greek children.

Find:

- **The spinning top made of clay. You had to hit it with a thread on the end of a stick to make it go round.**

- **The baby's bottle. The writing on the side says 'Drink, don't drop!'**

- **The little jug. It was the custom to give one to every child aged between three and four on a special day called 'Jugs' when they would have their first taste of wine. It was an important day for them.**

- **The clay doll with moving arms and legs.**

- **The rattle made of clay in the shape of a pig.**

Here is a baby on its pot.

Can you see how the pot works?

Babies who lived for more than ten days were given their name. This was an important day for the family.

Going to school

Greek boys had to learn to read and write, to play music and to remember famous stories like the story of Odysseus.

Here are two boys at school. One is learning to play a flute with two pipes. It was a bit like two recorders. The other has learnt something by heart and is saying it back to the teacher. The man with the stick is the slave who looks after one of the boys.

This is the alphabet that the boys used for reading and writing.

Δ	B	Γ	Δ	E	Z	H	Θ	I	K	Λ	M
(A)	(B)	(G)	(D)	(E)	(Z)	(EE)	(TH)	(I)	(K)	(L)	(M)

N	Ξ	O	Γ	P	S	T	Y	Φ	X	Ψ	Ω
(N)	(KS)	(O)	(P)	(R)	(S)	(T)	(U)	(PH)	(CH)	(PS)	(OH)

Girls did not go to school. Their mothers taught them.
A young girl learnt how to spin, weave and help on the farm while she waited to get married. She had to marry whoever her father chose.

Here is a wedding. In the evening the bridegroom came to the bride's house. He took her to his family's house in a cart, with the best man sitting on the back.

His mother met them at the door. She carried torches to light them in.

At home

Most Greek families had slaves to help with the hard work. Here are some slaves with their mistresses. Slaves could not do what they liked. They belonged to the people for whom they worked.

The slaves are wearing simpler clothes than the ladies they serve.

Which are the slaves?

This picture tells you a lot about the things that belonged to rich people.

Find:
- Two mirrors
- A chair with a back
- A stool
- Jewellery
- Two boxes for storing things
- A footstool with a sloping top
- A tall jar (on the footstool)
- A lamp (next to the jar)

Find the child slave who is doing up her mistresses' sandal.

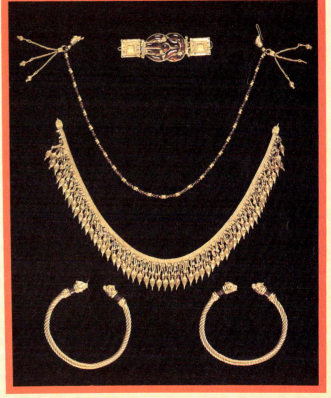

This jewellery belonged to a wealthy lady.

Find:
- The clasp for doing up her cloak at the shoulder
- Two necklaces
- Two arm-bracelets

Look at these two perfume bottles made out of clay in the shape of feet with sandals. What are the differences between the sandals?

One room of a Greek house was always set aside for the women to use for spinning and weaving wool. They made clothes for all the family and often some to sell as well. Most families owned at least one sheep to provide the wool.

The women did several different jobs.
See if you can find them:

- Weighing the wool.
- Pulling the wool out into a long twisted piece ready for spinning.
- Spinning the wool into a thin thread.
- Weaving the thread to make a piece of cloth.
- Folding finished pieces of cloth.

Are there any clues to tell you which lady was the mistress of the house and in charge of the work?

Here are some of the things the women used for spinning and weaving. The basket is a clay model. The real one was made of straw. Look again at the women working. What did they use it for?

Other things used for spinning were a silver rod called a 'distaff', a wooden stick called a 'spindle', and three 'whorls' made of clay.
On the next page you can see someone using them.

This picture of a woman spinning comes from a wine jug.

She puts the wool to be spun on the distaff and holds it in her left hand.
She pulls the wool out with her right hand.
The spindle on the end of the wool spins round and twists it into a thread.
The whorl at the bottom of the spindle keeps it steady and helps it to spin.
When the thread gets so long that it touches the ground, she winds it round the spindle and carries on.

Here is a woman spinning in Greece today. Look at the wine jug picture again. What do these pictures tell you has stayed the same in Greece since ancient times? What has changed?

Greek houses did not have taps or running water.
The women fetched water from a public fountain.

The water is coming out of a spout with a lion head. Two women have filled their jars and are going home. Two more have just arrived.
Which are they?

Usually slaves fetched the water, but these women are too well dressed to be slaves. Look at their clothes. They are made of wool. You can see what clever patterns Greek women could weave.

This girl is getting dressed. She is tying a belt round her waist. How does she hold her robe up while she does it?

Look at the women at the fountain again.
Is this girl wearing the same? What is different?

This girl is going to wash.

Find:

- **Her clothes**
- **The wash basin**
- **The water container**

They always washed in cold water.

The men used one room in the house to entertain guests. The women in the family never went to these parties. The guests lay on couches and the food was laid out on tables beside them. They drank wine mixed with water.

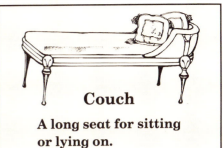

Couch

A long seat for sitting or lying on.

Find the wide drinking cups that they used.

They paid a cook to prepare a special meal for the party. He usually had his own outdoor oven. It was a bit like a modern barbecue.

Here are some of the things that they used for cooking.

Find:

- A cake-tray
- A ladle
- A strainer, with little holes in the bottom
- A small cooking pot
- A crusher, with a round end for crushing nuts or garlic

Usually the Greeks ate simple food which they could grow or catch themselves. They liked olives, lentils, onions, garlic, bread, cheese, yoghurt, fish, honey, apples, dates, figs and nuts. We still eat all these things today. Meat was expensive so they had it only on special occasions.

Making a living

Greek families grew their own food.

**How many different jobs can you see?
What are they?**

**How many different animals can you see?
What are they doing?**

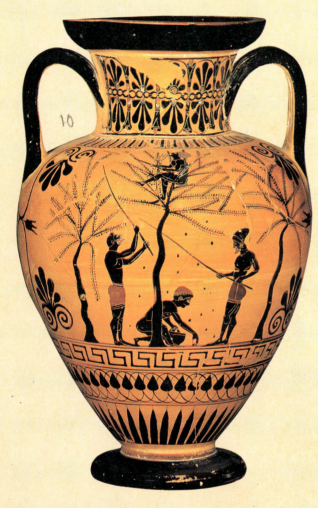

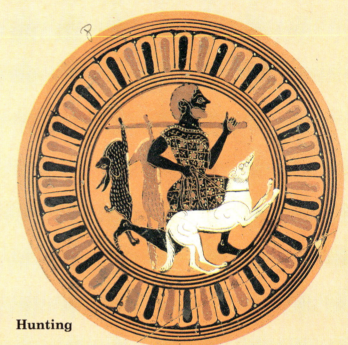

Hunting

**These men are picking olives.
How are they getting them out of the tree?
You can eat olives or you can crush them
to make olive oil. The Greeks used olive
oil for cooking and for burning in lamps.**

Fishing

What else did the Greeks eat?

Some people worked in little shops in the city.

What is this man making? Look round the edge of the picture for clues.

Here is a woman painting a vase in a pottery shop. Slaves did not usually wear their hair in that style, so she is not a slave. What does this clue tell you about Greek women?

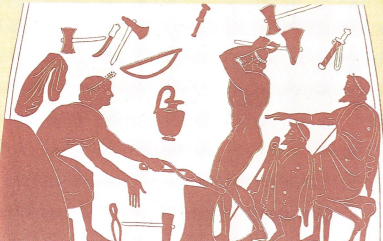

These are blacksmiths. They make things out of iron. You can see some of the things they have made on the wall. The man on the left is sitting by a hot furnace for heating up the iron. He has just taken a piece out for the other man to beat into shape. What tools are they using?

The two men sitting on the right may be customers, or they may own the shop. If they do, the two workers are probably slaves. We do not really know. Slaves did most of the really hard work.

Gods and Festivals

The Games

Every four years men and women athletes
from all over the world meet to take
part in the Olympic Games.

In 1996 our Olympic games will be a hundred years old and
will be held in Atlanta in the U.S.A.
The first games of modern times were held in Athens in 1896.

The Greeks invented the Olympic Games in ancient times.
They held them every four years for over a
thousand years in a Greek town called Olympia.
That is how they got their name.

This is the Olympic Stadium in Seoul in South Korea. Is it the same shape as the one in Olympia?

Stadium

A place for athletes to run races. There are seats all round so that people can watch.

This is a statue of Zeus. There was one like this inside the temple. It was made of gold and ivory. It was thirteen metres high.

This is a model of Òlympia.

Find:

- The running track. People watched from the slopes around it.

- The big courtyard with two clumps of trees in the middle (top left). This was where the athletes trained. It was called the 'Gymnasium'.

- The big temple in the middle. This was for the King of the Gods, called Zeus. The ancient Olympic games were held in honour of Zeus.

These people are welcoming home an athlete who has won in the Olympic Games.

Find:

- The wreath round his head. Every winner was given a wreath as a prize. It was made from the branch of an olive tree that grew beside the Temple of Zeus

- The crowd

- The flute player

- The entertainer

- The worker

It was a great honour to win. Only Greek people could take part. They came from all parts of the Greek lands. Every city wanted to be overall winner.

The Games were so important that if two cities were at war they had to stop fighting while the games were on.

There were two sets of Olympic Games, one for men and one for women.

This is a Spartan girl running in a race.

This is all that is left of the tunnel into the stadium at Olympia. The athletes came through here before each race. Imagine waiting in the tunnel before the start of your race.

This is the starting line for races. It has grooves for the runners' toes. Before they built this, the Greeks used to scratch a starting line in the sand. That's why some people talk about 'starting from scratch'.

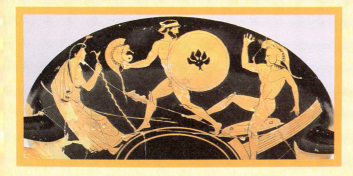

Here is a judge watching two athletes coming past the finishing post. They are running in the 'race in armour'.

Look at the picture. What did they have to do to win the race?

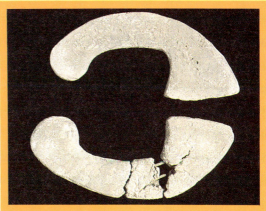

This is the long-jump. The man with the stick is an umpire. He measures the length of the jump. Can you see what the jumper is holding?

He is holding these. They are lead weights. The jumper had to swing them to help him go further. We don't know if the Greeks jumped from standing still or with a run up like athletes today.

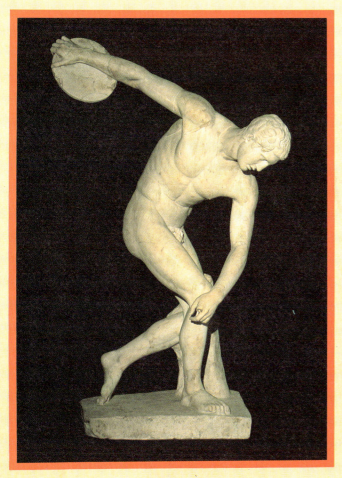

Throwing the discus

Wrestling

Gods and godesses

This is Mount Olympus. It is the highest mountain in Greece. The Greeks believed that Zeus, the King of the Gods, lived on the top with the other gods.

The Greeks thought of the gods as super-humans who lived as a family up on Mount Olympus. They made friends and quarrelled just like humans, but they never died.

Each god had a special job to do in the world.

The Greeks believed that the gods could make things go well or badly for humans, so they wanted to please them. That is why they gave them offerings of food and drink.

These Greeks have killed an animal. Now they are giving some of the meat to the god Apollo. This is called a sacrifice.

Find:

■ **The statue of Apollo**

■ **The stone table in front of it, called an altar**

■ **The boy carrying more meat on the end of sticks. They are going to eat it at a feast.**

Sacrifice

A gift offered to a god

This is a statue of Athena. She was the goddess of arts and crafts and making things. She was also the goddess of Athens.

An Athenian artist made the statue to go in a special temple in Athens, called the Parthenon. He made it of gold and ivory. It is about thirteen metres high.

Every year the Athenians made a new robe for the statue. They took it to the Parthenon in a big, noisy procession with musicians and people carrying cakes and olive branches.

The artist who made the statue of Athena also made a carving of the procession out of marble. These young men on horseback came at the end. The carving went all round the outside of the Parthenon.

The Athenians took lots of young bulls into the procession. Afterwards they sacrificed them and had a great feast with singing, dancing and story-telling.

The Theatre

The Greeks built this theatre in ancient times. They chose a hill and made a level place for the actors. Then they built seats into the hillside. Thousands of people could sit there.

Even though it is so big you can hear everything. If someone at the bottom drops a little stone you can hear it at the top.

Archaeologists have used clues from the ruins to build the stage area of the theatre up again.

Find the gangways for the audience to go to their seats.

This is the same theatre a few years ago. Modern actors are showing people what a Greek play was like in ancient times.

Find:

- The audience
- The big circle where the actors in black are standing
- The stage at the back with steps

The actors in black are called the Chorus. They all move and speak together. They talk to the audience about what is going on and say what they feel about it.

The Chorus always stays in the circle. The main actors usually stay on the stage at the back.

The Chorus did not always have to play the part of people. In one play it had to be a crowd of frogs. In another it had to be birds.

It probably wore costumes like these.

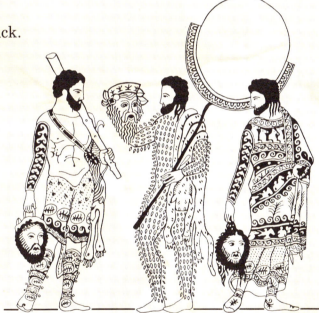

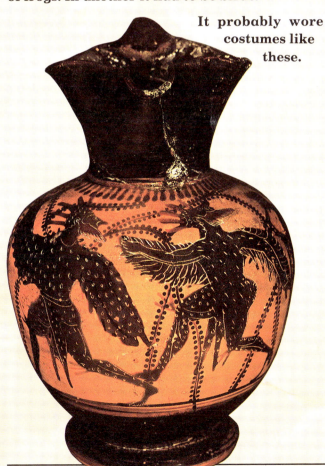

Here are three actors in their costumes. The one in the middle is wearing an all-in-one suit made of wool.

The one on the right is wearing the robes of a king from the East.

The one on the left is playing the part of the hero Herakles. He has a lion skin and a club.

The actors are holding masks. Greek actors always wore masks. No one acted without one. Men played the parts of men and women.

Here are two masks on a shelf. The Greeks usually made them of clay or cloth, sometimes of wood or metal. Look at the mouths. They are open and very big. That helps the actor's voice to sound loud.

The Greeks called serious plays 'tragedies' and funny plays 'comedies'.

Tragic actors had to move very slowly and smoothly, as if they were in a dance. When they were speaking they stood still in a fixed position like this.

Here is an actor in a tragedy.
Look at his mask.
What does it look like?

Greek comedies made fun of the heroes and the gods.

Here is Herakles trying to get the god Apollo to come down and help him. He is offering him some fruit and nuts in a basket. A slave is showing Apollo what a long way down it is.

Look at Apollo's costume. The actor is wearing a body-stocking with a padded fat-man costume over the top. He has ordinary stage clothes over that.

Here are two models of comic actors. What sort of people do you think they are meant to be?

Artists and Builders

A temple

This is the Parthenon, a temple which the Athenians built in about 420 BC
for the goddess Athena. It used to have lots of carvings on the outside.
Are there any left? A statue of Athena stood inside. Find the walls of
the room where it stood.

The tall stone posts that hold up the top of the
temple are called 'columns'. What clues are
there in the picture to tell you that the columns
were made of more than one piece of stone?
Can you work out roughly how many pieces?
The columns are not the same thickness all the
way up. What shape are they?

Do you think that the columns are standing
up completely straight?
The artist who designed the Parthenon worked
out that they look better if they sloped in a bit.
If you could draw a line from each column into
the sky, all the lines would meet five miles up.

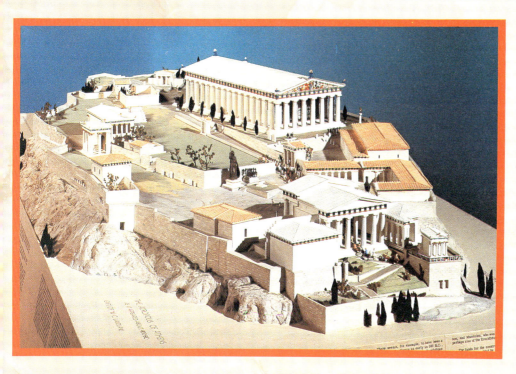

This model shows what the Parthenon and some of the buildings round it probably looked like when they were new buildings.

Archaeologists made the model using clues that they found from the ruins. Which bits have fallen down?

This shows you how the columns held up the top of the temple.

Find:

- The square stone at the top of each column.
- The stone blocks on top of the squares. How many are there?

Some of the buildings around us today look like buildings from ancient Greece.

These houses in Edinburgh, Scotland were built two hundred years ago.

What did the builders copy from Greek temples?

Try to find a building near your home that has bits copied from a Greek temple. Look at houses as well as at big buildings.

Lord Elgin and the Parthenon

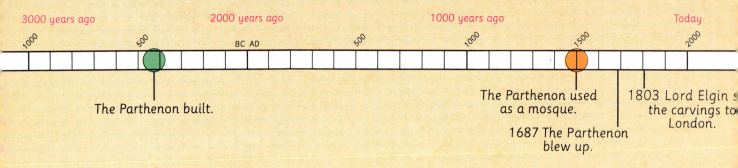

3000 years ago   2000 years ago   1000 years ago   Today

1000   500   BC AD   500   1000   1500   2000

The Parthenon built.

The Parthenon used as a mosque.

1687 The Parthenon blew up.

1803 Lord Elgin s the carvings to London.

About five hundred years ago the Greeks fought a war with the people of Turkey. The Turks won and became the rulers of Greece. The Turks belonged to the Muslim religion. A Muslim church is called a mosque. They turned the Parthenon into a mosque and they built a high tower.

VEDUTA DEL CAST D ACROPOLIS DALLA PARTE DI TRAMONTANA

About four hundred years ago, in 1687, the Parthenon blew up. An artist drew this picture afterwards.

The Turks kept their gunpowder in the Parthenon. An enemy shell hit it and the gunpowder exploded.

Some of the Parthenon stayed up but a lot of it was ruined. Some people started to take away bits of the stone to build their own homes.

This is Lord Elgin. He lived about two hundred years ago. He was interested in the carvings on the Parthenon. He knew they were very beautiful. Some had fallen down when the explosion happened. Some had stayed on the building.

Lord Elgin wanted artists in England to have a chance to see the carvings and learn about the way the Greeks did them.

The Turks said Lord Elgin could send some carvings to England.

This is one of the carvings he sent.

Instead of just saving the ones that had fallen he took some down from the Parthenon.

You can see them in the British Museum in London. There are so many that they have a big room all to themselves.

A few years ago the Greeks asked for the carvings back. They said they belonged to the Greek people, and should be in Athens not London.

What do you think?

Statues

Greek artists were very good at making statues.
These statues are all very different.

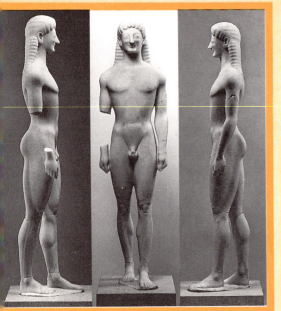

Do people usually stand like this?
Do you think the artist was trying to
show what a real person's body
looked like?

Is this the face of a real
person?
This is a statue of the
winner of a chariot race at
the Games.
What is different from the
first two?
Is anything the same?

600	500	400	300

Look at the bits of
colour on this statue.
The Greeks always
painted their statues
very brightly. Most of
the paint has now
rubbed off.
Was this artist
interested in how
clothes really look?

This is the
goddess of
beauty. What do
you think the
artist wanted to
show?

How is this
statue different
from the other
three?

Which do you
like best so far

44

This statue tells the story of a man who made the gods angry. While he was by the sea with his two sons the gods sent two sea-monsters to attack them. They coiled round the man and his sons who struggled to get free. But the monsters choked them to death and then slithered back into the sea.

Three artists made this statue. Why do you think they chose this story? What did they want the statue to show?

nother artist made this at about e same time. It is the gravestone a young man. Find:
The young man
His old father
His little slave boy
The dog
hat does each person seem to be inking and feeling?

200		100		BC	AD		100	

This is a god of love called Eros. He has wings. What clues are there to tell you that the artist watched a real little boy asleep and copied him?
What is different about this statue?
Is anything the same as the others?

Look at all the statues again.

What new things did Greek artists learn to do?

Scientists, Inventors and Doctors

Scientists and inventors

THE ARCHIMEDES SCREW

This is a machine for moving water from a low place to a high place.

It is like a very large corkscrew fixed in a pipe.
As you turn the handle the water is pushed up the pipe.
Can you work out how?

A Greek called Archimedes invented it.

ARCHIMEDES AND THE GOLDEN CROWN

One day a king came to Archimedes. He wanted to know if his crown was made of pure gold. He thought that there was another metal mixed in with it. The king knew how to find out.

1 Every metal has a different weight. So first he had to melt his crown and make it into a block of metal.

2 Then he had to take some pure gold and make it into a block exactly the same size.

3 Then he had to weigh each block.

4 If they were different weights it meant the crown was not pure gold.

The king did not want to melt his crown because it would spoil it. So he asked Archimedes if there was another way of finding out how much metal was in it.

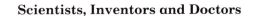

EUREKA!

When Archimedes was in the public baths he suddenly thought of the answer.

He was so excited that he ran home without any clothes on shouting 'I've found it.'

Archimedes told the king what to do.

1 'Take a bowl of water and mark the level.

water level

2 Then put in the crown. It will push the water up. Mark the new level.

new water level

old water level

3 Pour the water into another bowl until it is back to the first level.

4 The water in the second bowl is how much the crown pushed away. It takes up the same space as the crown.

So now you know how much metal is in the crown.

We still use Archimedes' idea to work out how much space things take up.
Next time you have a bath see how far your body pushes the water up the side of the bath.

The Greeks were also interested in numbers and shapes. A man called Euclid enjoyed working out all the things that you can do with straight lines and circles.

Euclid found things out about lines, circles, triangles, squares and rectangles. We still use his ideas today.

Doctors

The Greeks were interested in what made people well again if they were ill or wounded in battle.

Here is a soldier bandaging his friend's wound.

This child has a swollen tummy. What is the doctor doing?

The most famous Greek doctor was called Hippocrates. He was the first person to look carefully at people who were ill and write down what he saw. That way he found out a lot about diseases and how to make people better.

Before that people had tried to use magic to make them better. Hippocrates said that doctors should have nothing to do with magic.